Old DYSART
And East Kirkcaldy
by
Eric Eunson

CW00796817

A Dysart Sunday school outing aboard John Westwater's charabanc in the mid-1920s. The vehicle was an imported American REO; short for Ransom E. Olds, whose company also built Oldsmobile motor cars. Incidentally, the 1980s 'soft rock' group REO Speedwagon took its name from another 1920s model of bus made by the company.

© Eric Eunson 1998

First published in the United Kingdom, 1998,
by Stenlake Publishing, Ochiltree Sawmill, The Lade,
Ochiltree, Ayrshire, KA18 2NX
Telephone / Fax: 01290 423114

ISBN 1 84033 051 1

ACKNOWLEDGEMENTS

The author would like to thank the staff of the Reference Section of Kirkcaldy Central Library for their valuable assistance; Bill Fiet of Leslie for help with additional research and the use of the photographs on pages 6, 19, 23, 28, 29, 35, 38, and the front cover, and Robert Grieves of Paisley for the picture on the title page.

THE PUBLISHERS REGRET THAT THEY CANNOT SUPPLY
COPIES OF ANY PICTURES FEATURED IN THIS BOOK.

BIBLIOGRAPHY

Robert Brodie, *Reminiscences of Pathhead and Vicinity*, 1863
John Gifford, *The Buildings of Scotland, Fife*, 1988
A.J.G. MacKay, *Fife and Kinross*, 1896
Augustus Muir, *The Fife Coal Company Ltd.*, 1946
Owen Silver, *The Roads of Fife*, 1987
Jim Swan and Carol McNeill, *Dysart, A Royal Burgh*, 1997
C.A. Whatley, *That Important and Necessary Article*, 1984
James Wilkie, *The History of Fife*, 1923
Statistical Accounts, Parish of Dysart, entries dated 1792, 1836 and 1951.

INTRODUCTION

This book is concerned not just with the old burgh of Dysart, but also with those parts of modern Kirkcaldy which lay within Dysart parish, namely the former villages of Pathhead, Sinclairtown and Gallatown. Two explanations for the origin of the name Dysart prevail, one that it comes from the Celtic *dys-ard* or 'height of God'; the other that it derives from the Latin word *deserta*, meaning the fasting place of a holy man. Either interpretation alludes to the associations of the place with Saint Serf (also styled Cyre, Sair and in Latin *servanus*), one of the earliest figures of the Christian church of the Picts. Saint Serf is said to have died at an advanced age in the year 543 at the monastery he founded at Culross, where his remains are traditionally said to have been laid to rest. In the grounds of Dysart House, home to a closed order of Carmelite Nuns since 1930, a twin chambered cave is identified as Serf's *deserta*, where it is said he would retire for lengthy intervals in solitary meditation and prayer, as was the custom of missionaries of that age.

Typically, the earliest mention of Dysart concerns its church and is found in a document dated 1220, which reveals that Kirkcaldy had only a subordinate chapel of Dysart Kirk. The next reference to Dysart Kirk is its reconsecration by Bishop David de Bernham of St Andrews in 1245.

The St Clair or Sinclair family are first noted as feudal superiors of Dysart in 1407, although their influence is thought to date back to the reign of Malcolm IV (1153-1165) who granted many Fife estates to his Norman followers. They had Dysart elevated to the status of a burgh of barony some time before 1483. Around this date Dysart boasted around fifty small sailing vessels, engaged in a flourishing trade which included exports of salt, fish, hides and fleece.

In 1532 the assessed taxes for Dysart were half as great again as those of Kirkcaldy, indicating the relative importance of the two towns. However, the first half of the sixteenth century brought many tribulations to Dysart. The burgh was damaged by an English raid around 1501 and was again bombarded by an English fleet in 1522. In 1559 Scotland was divided by war between the Catholic regent, Mary of Lorraine, and the Protestant nobility. Dysart was sympathetic to the Protestant cause and was held by the Lords of the Congregation, led by the Earl of Arran. In the closing months of 1559 Dysart fell to the French, who looted and occupied the burgh for a time. The French were forced to retreat early in 1560 when an English fleet sent to support the Scots Protestants appeared in the Forth and severed the enemy's links with their main army at Leith.

Dysart's fortunes began to turn again in the years immediately following the Reformation. Salt-making began to become a staple industry (salt is first recorded as being exported from the town in 1330) and Dysart remained an important supplier of this commodity to both foreign and domestic markets until the early nineteenth century. Until potatoes and turnips began to be grown as winter feed crops for livestock in the late eighteenth century, most farm animals were slaughtered in late autumn and their carcasses preserved in salt. Before the discovery of rock salt in Cheshire in the 1720s the only means of making salt was by extracting it from sea water by evaporation, a lengthy process which required six tons of small coal to produce one ton of sea salt. In view of this it is safe to assume that Dysart can also trace the working of its coal reserves to the fourteenth century. In 1574 the town boasted sixteen salt pans. The pans themselves were shallow iron troughs, rectangular in shape and contained within custom-built panhouses on the foreshore.

The period from 1570 to 1630 saw the peak of the salt trade between the Forth ports and customers in the Netherlands and the Baltic. In Dysart this trade was so brisk that it earned the epithet 'Little Holland', a nickname reflected in the Dutch influence on its architecture from this period. Dysart is first represented in Parliament in 1594. This privilege was normally reserved for royal burghs, although no documents are known to exist to prove that Dysart ever received a formal grant of this title. The town may have owed its status to its commercial importance.

One peril that constantly faced sea ports was the arrival of epidemics from visiting ships. Dysart was ravaged by plagues, probably cholera or typhus, in the years 1564, 1579 and 1584, the last of which claimed four hundred lives. During the early seventeenth century the shipping lanes of the North Sea were plagued by French pirates and Dysart lost thirty-six merchant vessels to the plunderers. To its discredit, the burgh fell prey to the hysteria of witch-hunting which affected many places in Scotland during the seventeenth century. Very few details survive, but trials are said to have taken place in 1626-27, 1630 and 1643-44. On the second of these occasions eighteen women and one man were tried along with an unknown number of others from West Wemyss. Some were found guilty and burned at the Red Rocks to the east of the town, but the number of victims is unknown.

Dysart suffered badly in the Wars of the Covenant in 1644-45 and it was reported in 1691 that during these years 'the most part of the skippers and traffiquers were killed'. A further outbreak of plague in 1648 was followed by an occupation by the soldiers of Oliver Cromwell from 1651-56. Recovery from this catalogue of catastrophe began to be apparent in the early eighteenth century. Between 1715 and 1719 the saltworks produced an average of 558 tons per annum, a figure exceeded only by the Earl of Wemyss' pans at West Wemyss. This represents an annual consumption of 3,348 tons of local coal by the Dysart pans. The Dutch trade was virtually wiped out after 1640 by wars in Europe, but Baltic customers continued to provide a ready market for Dysart salt. This market too began to decline rapidly after 1740, but a domestic trade developed with customers in Dundee and Perth which assured the survival of the industry. Despite this, the salt industry was approaching a period of decline. In 1792 Dysart had only seven pans and output had fallen to around half of what it had been in 1715. Salt had been subject to heavy taxation since 1713 and this had maintained high prices; the abolition of the salt tax in 1823 led to the eventual demise of the industry.

Coal working at Dysart began to expand after 1750, notably with the sinking of the Engine Pit, later named Lady Blanche, above the Pan Ha' in 1753. Three years later a new colliery village was begun at the Boreland, lying midway between the new Engine Pit and the indeterminately old workings of the pit latterly known as the Randolph Colliery. In 1792 the Boreland housed 196 people, by 1816 this had risen to 300, but had fallen back to 184 twenty years later. The Dysart coals were very prone to spontaneous ignition and were said to set themselves alight on average every forty years. A major fire was reported in 1662 and in 1700 flames could be seen at night emitting from pit mouths near the shore. Another pit was accidentally set on fire in 1741 by sparks from a neighbouring lime kiln.

The 1750s marked a significant revival of foreign trade in Dysart and in 1756 several merchants in the burgh began to import wine and spirits in their own vessels. Handloom weaving of linen was introduced to the parish between 1710 and 1720 and by the end of the century had largely replaced nail making as the staple employment in the villages of Pathhead and Gallatown. Initially the weavers were entirely self employed and sold their wares at annual 'white cloth' fairs held in Dysart, Pathhead and Gallatown, which were visited by merchants from Edinburgh and Glasgow. As the century progressed more and more weavers entered into contracts with larger manufacturers to supply them with finished work and the cloth fairs were virtually defunct by 1790. In 1792 there were an estimated 700-750 looms employing around 5,000 hands, of whom about half were thought to live outwith the parish boundaries. At the same date Dysart owned twenty-three square rigged vessels and two sloops with combined crew of 249 men. Most sailed to the Baltic with coal or ballast and returned with wood and other articles which were delivered to Leith, Dundee and Perth. Also in 1792, Dysart was served by a weekly passage boat to Leith. A weekly steamer service between Largo, Dysart and the Chain Pier at Newhaven provided by the paddle steamer *Royal George* was instituted in 1824, this was upgraded to a daily service, provided by the *Victory*, in 1826. The Largo, Leven and Dysart passage remained an important ferry until 1857, although the Dysart part of the service declined in importance after the arrival of the railway there in 1847.

During the early nineteenth century handloom weaving declined as the manufacture was transferred to factories, and in 1836 it was said that the cottage industry was virtually extinct in the parish. In 1809 James Normand took over a small linen manufactory in Dysart and his enterprise proved so successful that he built a large factory equipped with the town's first power looms in the early 1850s. A neighbouring power loom factory was opened by J. & A. Terrace in 1867.

Michael Nairn introduced the manufacture of floorcloth to Pathhead on the western edge of the parish in 1847 and began making linoleum in the 1860s. The success of this industry brought prosperity and expansion to Kirkcaldy and its neighbouring villages. Dysart and Kirkcaldy had long rivalled one another in importance but as new industries were introduced Kirkcaldy emerged as the more dynamic town. By 1870 the burgh of Dysart was still virtually contained within its compact medieval boundaries; Kirkcaldy by contrast was built right to its burgh limits and included a sprawl of industry and housing that had turned Pathhead and its neighbours into one built-up mass. In 1876 most of Dysart parish, including Pathhead, Sinclairtown and Gallatown, was annexed by Kirkcaldy, along with much of the parish of Abbotshall, including Linktown.

Dysart was hit by heavy job losses in the 1920s following the closure of Normand's textile mill in 1922 and the Lady Blanche Colliery in 1928. Coal from both the Frances and Randolph Collieries was transported by rail, but coal from the Lady Blanche was shipped through Dysart Harbour as the pit was surrounded by the town on its landward side. Duty on these shipments provided a valuable income for the burgh treasury and their loss plunged the town council into financial crisis. Dysart had stubbornly resisted annexation by Kirkcaldy for many years but was forced to surrender and merged with its old rival in 1930.

Dysart's first council houses were completed in 1921 in Normand Road and Hill Street. Further small schemes were added to the east and north of the town in the 1930s, but after the Second World War Dysart still contained many houses without modern sanitation. Councillors demanded comprehensive redevelopment in 1953 and demolition work started in the lower part of the town in 1957. In 1958 the east end of Victoria Street was cleared and a square of new houses erected to designs by Wheeler and Sproson, winning the partnership the prestigious Saltire Award in 1960.

But the redevelopment of Dysart had many critics. Many people displaced by so-called slum clearance were refused new housing in the old burgh and were sent to schemes in other parts of Kirkcaldy, far from their friends and work. Others complained that the new houses had only expensive electric heating, ill-suited to a community largely made up of miners whose income was supplemented by a coal allowance from their employers. Agitation to preserve some part of the antique town began in the mid-1960s, culminating in the restoration of the Pan Ha' by the National Trust for Scotland in 1968-69. Dysart today is a sadly dismembered place, its showpieces of antiquity hemmed in by the geometric vision of sixties planners. However, despite nearly seventy years as an annexe of Kirkcaldy, and crippling job losses inflicted by the collapse of Fife's mining industry in the 1980s, Dysart retains a spirit of independence and pride that shows no sign of abating.

The Francis Colliery was established by the Earl of Rosslyn around 1850. In 1896 the Fife Coal Company took over the pit and the change to the female form of the name 'Frances' appears to be contemporary with this event. Improvements were effected in 1927, including the installation of conveyors to carry the coal from the face. Conveyors were also introduced to the Randolph at the same time, but were soon removed when it was found that the old method of loading the coal into hutches by hand was cheaper. The pit-head shown in this 1920s photograph was shared by the Frances Colliery, sunk to deep workings, and the Frances Mine, which was reported in 1946 to run at a gradient of one in four for a distance of 700 yards into deposits of Lower Dysart Coal. The Frances was always a wet pit and this earned it the nickname of 'The Dubbie', from the Scots' word 'dub' meaning a pool of dirty water. Corrosive acidic water had to be pumped from the shallower workings, while the seepage into the deep parts of the pit was strongly alkaline. In 1946 over 230,000 gallons of water were pumped out of the pit and colliery every day. When the mines were nationalised on 31 December 1946, the Frances employed 700 men and had an average daily output of 1,100 tons of coal. An attempt to extend the workings under the Firth of Forth in 1937 proved successful and by 1958 these stretched three-quarters of a mile out to sea and were among the most productive in the country. By this date 1,400 men were employed and daily output had increased to 2,000 tons. In the late 1970s the workings were joined to those of the Michael Colliery at East Wemyss, closed after a disastrous fire in 1967, and in 1980 a £10 million link with the Seafield Colliery was completed. The national miners' strike started in March 1984 and underground fires raged through the idle workings. In February 1985 British Coal announced the Frances was to close with the loss of 500 jobs. Locals campaigning to have the Dubbie preserved as a mining museum were unsuccessful and demolition of the pit-head buildings began in 1994.

When this 1905 picture was taken Dysart had golden sands and the Dubbie Braes were a popular place for recreation. The whole area was given a facelift in 1887 as part of the town's celebrations for Queen Victoria's Golden Jubilee. This included the erection of a bandstand, which stood behind the boys in the foreground.

The Dubbie Braes Dysart.

M. 115.

From the outset redd (waste) from the Dubbie was simply dumped onto the braes, and by the time this early 1930s postcard was published the amenity of the foreshore was already under threat. By the 1950s the footpath which had once linked Dysart and West Wemyss was completely buried, and the harbour was threatened with extinction as the sea washed waste from the skirts of the bing along the coast. Coastal dumping had already destroyed Buckhaven Harbour and rendered East Wemyss prone to flooding, yet it was allowed to continue for more than twenty years. Although Dysart has been denied its mining museum, the environmental legacy of the industry serves as a constant memorial.

THE PIPERS BRAE, DYSART.

1041 SB.

The area known as the Piper's Braes was formerly the Bow Butts, where the men of seventeenth century Dysart gathered for archery practice. Later the land was granted to the burgh's piper to graze his livestock. The curved row of houses on the lower right of this late 1930s view was Dovecot Crescent, built by James Normand to house workers at his nearby linen mill. The row was abandoned by the 1960s and in 1966 the National Coal Board took over the site to extend dumping from the Frances Colliery.

In 1450 Dysart had no man-made harbour and ships were grounded in front of the Pan Ha' at low tide. Sometime thereafter a natural skerry of rocks to the east was incorporated into a pier, but the 'East Haven of Dysart' had fallen into such disrepair by 1615 that it was abandoned. Work on the east and west piers enclosing the outer dock of the present harbour began around the same date. Plans for extensive improvements were prepared in 1819 by the civil engineer Robert Stevenson. These included the development of an inner basin incorporating a large quarry at the harbour head and the extension of the east pier to improve access for the ferry steamers. Work on the scheme began in 1829 and took two years to complete. The new inner harbour was closed by dock gates, which meant that ships could be loaded with coal at any state of the tide, the first port on Scotland's east coast to possess such a facility. The accompanying picture of the outer harbour dates from around 1900.

Dysart Harbour.

The large building in the background of this 1930 view was built in 1835 by Dysart Town Council, and was intended for use as a shed for boiling whale blubber to extract oil. It was a speculative venture, rather like a modern advance factory, and was intended to exploit the growth of Kirkcaldy's whaling fleet. However, Lord Rosslyn of Dysart House was horrified at the prospect of noxious fumes from the factory and, despite assurances from the town council that his fears were groundless, he applied for an interim interdict to halt its construction. The battle eventually went to the House of Lords who upheld the Earl's wishes, and although the building was completed it never served its intended purpose. The oil shed that never was is now home to Dysart Sailing Club.

The Harbour, Dysart.   M 115.

Although Dysart's staple industry was coal mining by the time this late 1920s picture was taken, the flotilla of small craft in the foreground serve as a reminder of its maritime tradition. Many miners had small fishing boats and these doubled as racing yawls during the annual regattas, which were already long established by the 1870s. In addition Dysart also had some twenty-five custom built racing yawls, built between 1911 and 1953. A larger fishing boat in the background has been hauled up for repair on the slipway of the then disused shipyard. A ship's carpenter settled in the burgh in 1764 and by 1792 had built forty-three merchant vessels, fifteen of them for Dysart owners. The business was taken over in the 1860s by John Watt, a Dundee man, but despite surviving a trade depression in the late 1870s he sold the concern to Foster Brothers in 1884. They attempted to revive the yard, but disposed of it after only five years. The ailing yard was finally closed shortly before the Great War.

The Pan Ha' takes its name from the strip of land above the high water mark where some of Dysart's panhouses stood. Two stood in front of the buildings on the right of this picture and another three were immediately around the corner. A map of 1821 shows that they had rounded gables to the sea to deflect wind and reduce the risk of storm damage. However, by the time this view was taken around 1900 the site of these buildings had been eroded by the sea. The Pan Ha' was restored in 1968-69 by the architect W. Schomberg Scott under the supervision of the National Trust for Scotland as part of their 'Little Houses' programme. Bay House, left, is the oldest of the group and was built for Patrick Sinclair in the sixteenth century. A stone over a doorway into the garden is dated 1583 but this is believed to have come from the old manse which once stood in the grounds. During the heyday of the ferry traffic in the early nineteenth century Bay House became the Bay Horse Inn, closing around 1900. The two storey house to the right was demolished *c.*1930 but the other buildings, all dating from the mid-eighteenth century, have been restored.

Mid-eighteenth century house at the foot of the Hie Gait, photographed *c*.1910.

The eighty foot tower of St Serf's Church was built in the early sixteenth century, and its gun-loops and impressive proportions reveal that it was built as much for the defence of the prosperous burgh as to embellish the church. The adjoining church dated from before the Reformation, but was described in 1792 by Rev. John Muirhead as being dark and having low side walls. The old kirk was finally replaced in 1802 by the Barony Kirk at the Townhead and two years later most of its predecessor was demolished to create a new road from the Engine Pit to the harbour.

Dysart Cross in 1905, looking into Cross Street with Andrew Forrester's chemist's shop on the left and David Owler's newsagent's on the right hand corner. This area was the burgh's market place from medieval times and in 1792 there were four annual fairs held here: 'one for linseed [more properly described as flax, which was spun and woven into linen]; one for white cloth; another for wool and white cloth, and one for black cattle'. These fairs were already in decline by this date and had virtually ceased by the 1830s.

HIGH STREET FROM THE CROSS, DYSART.

92343 (JV)

Fortunately the Cross was spared the worst excesses of redevelopment and all the seventeenth and eighteenth century buildings in the foreground of this 1924 view remain today. The ornamental lamp standard was erected in 1887 in honour of Queen Victoria's Golden Jubilee. The burgh also marked this event by building new council chambers, designed by Glasgow architects Campbell, Douglas and Sellars, next to the tolbooth.

The lower part of the tolbooth, on the left of this 1905 picture, dates from 1576. The forestair adjoining the west gable was added in 1617. In 1656 the upper part of the building was used as a magazine by the occupying forces of Oliver Cromwell. A soldier guarding the gunpowder carelessly discarded a match and the resulting explosion wrecked the building. It remained in a partly ruined condition until 1707 when it was reconstructed in its present form.

A Mechanics' Institute and associated library were founded in Dysart in 1849 and moved into these custom built premises designed by James Aitken in 1874. This 1905 postcard was published by A.T. Buist, the town's sub-postmaster, whose premises occupied the right hand part of the ground floor of the institute. A post office existed at least as early as 1755, when Dysart possessed the status of a post town. This was the highest grade of office and meant that it sent mails directly to, and received them from, Edinburgh. The Dysart office was downgraded to an independent sub office under the jurisdiction of Kirkcaldy on 24 March 1825, an event which reflects the gradual decline of the town's importance.

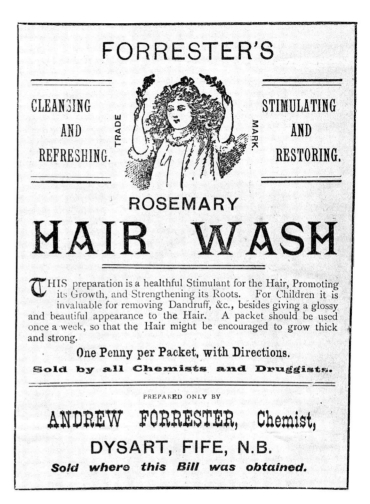

The Reverend William Muir was minister of Dysart's Barony Church from 1850-65. Like many of his profession he was a keen amateur historian and wrote a book entitled *The Antiquities of Dysart* in 1855. This *carte-de-visite* photograph was taken by John Nisbet of Kirkcaldy and dates from around 1865.

A handbill dating from the turn of the century proclaiming the virtues of Andrew Forrester's patent shampoo - wash your hair once a week, whether it needs it or not!

The church retained control over education in Scotland until the passing of the 1872 Education Act. This transferred responsibility for schools to independent local school boards and also abolished tuition charges, which had always existed under the old system. The 1872 Act also stipulated that school attendance was compulsory for every child between the ages of five and thirteen. At this time Dysart school was located at the east end of the High Street. The passing of the Act created an urgent need for further accommodation and a second school was built at the top of what is now School Street in 1873. These merged in 1881, when the High Street school became the infant department. Both were replaced by Blairhill School in Normand Road in 1915.

Cross Street, Dysart 8

Right: When war broke out in 1914, John Patterson of 23 Fraser Place, Dysart, worked as shaftsman at the Frances Colliery. He enlisted with the 7th Battalion of the Black Watch, later transferring to the Royal Field Artillery. On 26 August 1915 he was serving at La Boiselle in France, when an NCO went to explore an abandoned mine. He was quickly overcome by gas and fell to the bottom, whereupon a private went in after him to attempt a rescue. When he too failed to return, Patterson immediately descended after them. He was badly gassed himself, but was unable to save the two men and barely escaped with his life. His bravery won him the Distinguished Conduct Medal, which was presented to him before a large crowd in the Normand Hall on 22 February 1916. He was also awarded the Humane Society's Vellum.

Left: Cross Street in the late 1930s.

Normand Road. Dysart

At the end of the eighteenth century Dysart did not extend beyond the south side of the present main road through the town, comprising Townhead and Normand Road. The first building on the north side of the street was the Barony Parish Church of 1802. It was joined in 1867 by the United Presbyterian Church, on the right of this 1927 view. This building, with its top heavy steeple, was the work of Glasgow architect James Brown. The original name of the developing street was, unsurprisingly, Church Street but was later renamed in honour of Dysart's family of linen magnates.

The first record I can find of the Royal Hotel at Townhead dates from the late 1840s, when the innkeeper was David Dewar. The road through Dysart, Townhead and Boreland was upgraded to a turnpike in 1790, joining the contemporary main turnpike roads to Cupar and the East Neuk. The upgrading of the eastbound coast road to Leven and Wemyss began in 1807 and in 1840 a stone bridge was built at the mouth of the Leven. Previously the lowest bridge on the river had been at Cameron Bridge and the opening of this new crossing led to a sudden increase in the amount of traffic passing through Dysart. The opening of the Royal Hotel may be related to this event; in 1850 Dewar introduced a posting establishment where coaches could change horses. At the same time he began hiring gigs from his premises.

Alex and Maggie Shand were the proprietors of Dysart's Royal Hotel from around 1910 until the mid-1920s.

The first sod of the Edinburgh and Northern Railway's line from Burntisland to Ladybank, Cupar and Lindores, was cut at Kinghorn in 1846. The railway, which included the stations at Kirkcaldy, Sinclairtown and Dysart, was officially opened to traffic on 20 June 1847. On 17 May 1848 extensions were completed from Lindores to Perth and Cupar to Ferryport-on-Craig (Tayport). The name of the company was changed to the Edinburgh Perth and Dundee Railway the following year. The EP&DR was bought by the larger North British Railway Company in 1862, themselves taken over by the London and North Eastern Railway in 1923. The dismantling of Fife's rail network began soon after nationalisation in 1948 and Dysart Station was closed in 1968.

Watt Street, Dysart

The area between Normand Road and the railway line was developed between 1890 and 1900. Watt Street, photographed here in 1907 looking east into Terrace Street, was named in honour of John Watt, former owner of the Dysart shipyard and provost of the burgh from 1870 until his death in 1886.

GOLF HOUSE, DYSART.

Dysart Golf Club was instituted in 1897 and opened a nine hole course north of Dysart Cemetery in Windmill Road in March 1898. The clubhouse stood just off Loughborough Road and a new extension had just been completed on the right hand side of the building when this postcard was published in 1905. Part of the course was ploughed up and used to grow vegetables during the Second World War; and in the early 1950s the town council developed the former course with housing. The club itself remained in existence until 1963, when it was offered premises at the newly opened Municipal Golf Course at Dunnikier. However, so few members remained that this offer was never taken up and Dysart Golf Club was wound up in 1964.

RAVENSCRAIG CASTLE, KIRKCALDY

Work on Ravenscraig Castle began in 1460 in the first year of the reign of James III. It was intended as a home for his mother, Mary of Gueldres, widow of James II. The work was overseen by the King's Master of Works, David Boys, and the mason is believed to have been Henry Merlioun. Work was suspended in 1463 upon the death of the Queen Dowager and the first major stage may not have been completed until after 1470, when the castle was granted to William Sinclair, Earl of Caithness. It is thought to be the first castle in Scotland built to withstand bombardment by artillery. The west tower, on the left of this 1912 illustration, is believed to be the oldest part. The lower range on its right dates from the sixteenth century and is joined to the east tower, which was built in the seventeenth century when the castle's defences were strengthened. The ramparts were dismantled during the Cromwellian occupation in the 1650s and the castle is thought to have been abandoned at this time.

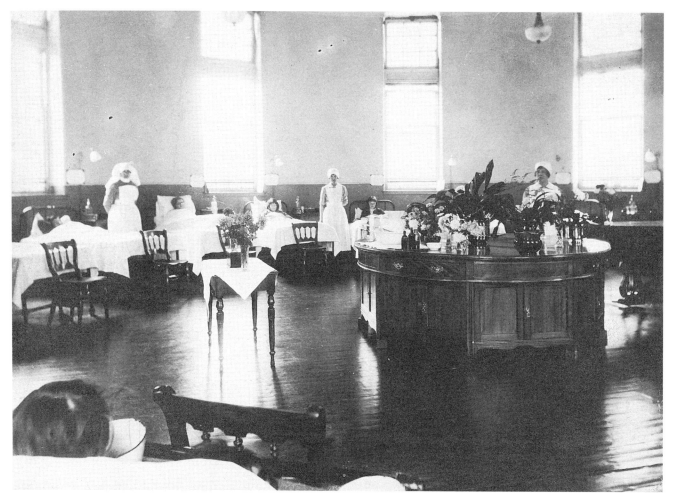

A turn of the century photograph of the interior of the round children's ward of Kirkcaldy Cottage Hospital in Nether Street. Its construction was funded by Michael Nairn and it opened in 1890. By the early 1950s it had become too small to serve the needs of the town, and Nairn proposed that a replacement should be built on a part of Ravenscraig Park he had earmarked for the purpose. However, this site was deemed unsuitable and it was the former Fever Hospital in Hayfield Road which was developed as the new Victoria Infirmary, the first part of which opened in 1961. The old Cottage Hospital stood empty from 1967 until its demolition in 1985.

Not a stone of Pathhead's Nether Street, as seen in this Edwardian view, looking west from the foot of St Clair Street, remains. The row of houses on the right dated from the seventeenth century. They were listed buildings and the council had to fight a lengthy appeal before tearing them down during the redevelopment of the area in 1964-65. The area is now occupied by the Ravenscraig tower blocks, designed by local architects Wheeler and Sproson and built by Wimpey Construction. Pathhead was created a burgh of barony under the superiority of John Watson of Dunnikier *c.*1690, and in 1695 an Act of Parliament granted it the right to hold two annual markets. During the eighteenth century peace brought prosperity to central Scotland; merchants increased in number and as they opened shops in the towns, so the importance of traditional street markets declined. By 1792 Pathhead's markets were minor affairs and by 1863 consisted of only a one day fair in October, when a handful of shoemakers set up their stalls in Mid Street.

Nether Street, Kirkcaldy.

Pathhead was formerly known as Dunnikier and developed on a detached portion of the estate of the same name. This estate is known to have existed at the time of the Battle of Flodden in 1513, and the first recorded feus in Pathhead were granted in 1582 by its owner, David Lundie of Balgonie. At the beginning of the nineteenth century Nether Street was surfaced with a mixture of stones gathered from the land and rounded, granite rocks brought into Dysart as ballast by trading ships from Aberdeen. In 1828 it was adopted by the trustees of the turnpike road from Kirkcaldy to Crail, who relaid it with cobbles and removed a number of projecting forestairs from houses fronting the street. The houses on the right of this 1905 postcard were demolished in 1964.

Only the white building on the left with its gable to the street survives from this 1950s picture of the west end of Nether Street. This was Dunnikier House, now Path House, built in 1692 for John Watson as a town residence to complement his country seat of the same name. It is inscribed with the initials of Watson and his wife Euphan Orrock. The pedimented building on the left housed the offices of Nairn's linoleum works which had extensive factories on both sides of the street. The oldest part was on the south side of the road, at the apex of the picture. It was built in 1847 by Michael Nairn for the manufacture of floorcloth, a product made by applying a treacly paint to stretched canvas. When Fred Walton, a Yorkshireman, invented linoleum in the 1860s, Nairn began making the new material. It proved to be a roaring success with the public and Nairn's quickly became the world's largest linoleum manufacturer.

By 1951 Nairn's operated seven linoleum factories in Kirkcaldy, one of which made floor cloth; the company also had a paper mill, and a canvas works at the harbour where the hessian backing for the lino was made. From the early 1960s the decline in demand was relentless and most of the Pathhead factories were demolished between 1967 and 1971. The Forbo Nairn group continued to make vinyl floor coverings at their remaining plant in Den Road and a recent surge in demand has led to the resumption of linoleum making. After an absence of twenty years the nostrils of Kirkcaldy can once again catch a whiff of that 'queer like smell'. This photograph was taken on the same day as the preceding illustration and both show my late uncle, William 'Pim' Fowler of East Wemyss, testing Fife Constabulary's first walkie-talkie. The occasion was the removal of the cobbles on Nether Street and the Path.

Only the street names remain to assist with locating this 1905 picture of Mid Street, looking east toward St Clair Street. The photographer was standing at the corner of Flesh Wynd, right, which continued on the other side of the street as Bogie's Wynd. The boundary between Pathhead and Sinclairtown, and the lands of the Oswalds of Dunnikier and the St Clairs of Dysart, was formerly marked by the Rymalton Burn, which flowed through the dip in the road visible in the background. This had been completely culverted by 1860, but its course followed the line of Broad Wynd and the east ends of both Mid Street and Commercial Street were feued as part of Sinclairtown. The tall building on the left of the picture was the back of the Pathhead Co-operative Society's premises which faced Commercial Street. Designed in 1905 by David Forbes-Smith, they were demolished in the late 1980s.

Mid Street, Kirkcaldy.

4077. 15

Another view of Mid Street in 1905, this time looking towards Kirkcaldy and taken a couple of doors west of the foot of Bogie's Wynd. Prior to 1800 many of these houses had forestairs, like the example in the left foreground, but most of these were subsequently removed during a programme of improvements, and by 1863 only around seventeen remained. Most of the houses in Mid Street and the warren of wynds and backlands that lay on either side of it were cleared away in 1964-65. One survivor was the Feuars' Arms pub in Bogie's Wynd, which stood alone in the middle of a wasteland for the next twenty-five years. Built around 1890, its exterior is unremarkable but it has a superb art nouveau interior with tiling by Doulton & Co. including what is possibly the only category 'A' listed gents' pub toilet in Scotland! Since 1990 this area has been redeveloped by Thomas Mitchell & Co. as Pathhead Garden Village. The name may be a bit twee, but this traditionally-inspired development is one of the most pleasing in Kirkcaldy in recent years.

Left: Until the introduction of handloom weaving in the early eighteenth century, Pathhead's principal industry was the manufacture of nails. This trade developed using old iron brought into Dysart as ballast on Dutch trading ships, and was facilitated by the ready availability of coal on the Dunnikier Estate. In 1792 there were still forty-three smiths in Pathhead, making an estimated six million nails per annum. The industry was virtually defunct by 1836, and John Hutchison of Mid Street was described as the last of the town's nailmakers when this picture was taken *c.*1895. He is wearing the uniform of a volunteer fireman and was attached to the nearby fire station in Church Street.

Right: Members of John Hutchison's family, photographed behind their house at the east end of Mid Street around 1905. On the extreme left is his widow Mary Hutchison and next to her their daughter, also Mary Hutchison. The baby in her arms is a cousin, William Horne, who many years later became harbour master at Dysart.

COMMERCIAL STREET, KIRKCALDY.

Before 1720 Mid Street and Nether Street comprised the whole of Pathhead, but in that year feuing began to the north along an old road known as the Back o' the Dykes. This was part of a thoroughfare known as the Mill Vennel, which led all the way from Dysart to Kirkcaldy's West Mill at Inverteil. Before the new street was developed every feuar on the north side of Mid Street had the privilege of a door in the north wall of their property as access to this road. The last feus in Back Street, later renamed Commercial Street, were granted in 1737. This 1905 picture was taken from outside the Pathhead Hall, completed in 1884 and designed by the Glasgow architects Campbell, Douglas and Sellars. This portion of Commercial Street was spared by the bulldozers and has since received some much needed refurbishment. In the background is Bank House on St Clair Street, a recent casualty of road widening.

An early iron wheeled lorry belonging to Douglas & Grant's Dunnikier Foundry in Den Road, photographed *c.*1910. The firm was founded by Robert Douglas (1822-92). A native of Kilbarchan in Renfrewshire, he came to Kirkcaldy and established the foundry in 1854. One of his first contracts was the making of shot and shells for the British army in the Crimea. In 1872 he took on his son-in-law Lewis Grant as a partner in the company. Machinery made at the works was exported to every corner of the globe; mills for the rice industry were a speciality, an example of which can be seen on the back of the truck.

The machine shop of the Dunnikier Foundry *c.*1905. Following the death of Lewis Grant in 1916, the business was taken over by his son Lewis C. Grant, but was forced to close in 1919. Lewis junior resurrected the company on a smaller scale in 1927, making only rice milling machinery. The firm was located in a former linen mill in East Quality Street, Dysart, and moved to new premises on the Mitchelston Industrial Estate in 1980. It now specialises in precision sheet metal work and engineering products for the electronics industry. The manufacture of rice milling machinery was discontinued in 1995.

The foot of Clair Street, photographed in 1903, showing the former Pathhead Free Church on the left. This was built in 1844 and was heightened in 1859, when the belfry was also added. After the Free Church and the Established Church were reunited in 1929 it became known as Pathhead West Church. When the congregations of Pathhead West and East Churches were united in 1958, the West Church was abandoned; it was demolished in 1963.

Considering the devastation road development has wrought on St Clair Street, the unprepossessing little church of the United Original Secessionists is an unexpected survivor. A congregation of seceders was formed in Pathhead in 1852, and met in an old house in Mid Street until they had amassed enough money to build this church in 1879. They were a strict sect and forbade the singing of anything other than the Psalms during worship. The seceders broke away from the Church of Scotland because they regarded it as too liberal for tolerating 'the profane diversions of the stage; together with night assemblies and balls - sinful occasions of wantonness and prodigality'. Only a dozen secession churches were still open when the sect decided to return to the Church of Scotland in 1956. Shortly afterwards their Kirkcaldy church was sold to the Apostolic Church, who occupy it to this day.

A North British Railway Company Wheatley goods locomotive, photographed at Sinclairtown Station *c*.1890. The station opened in 1847 on the route of the Edinburgh and Northern Railway. By 1904 branches from Sinclairtown led to the Dunnikier Colliery ('Pannie Pit'), Dunnikier Foundry and Kirkcaldy Harbour. The station was closed in 1968, but at the time of writing serious proposals are being considered to open a new station to serve east Kirkcaldy, either here or in Dysart.

St Clair Street was laid out in 1800 at the sole expense of James Sinclair, and was known as New Road until well into the nineteenth century. The redevelopment of Sinclairtown was first proposed in 1964, when it was found that 48% of the houses in the area had no scullery, bathroom or inside toilet. Some 300 householders were served with compulsory purchase orders but many resisted. A Public Enquiry was held in 1967 and the development plans were ratified by the Secretary of State for Scotland in 1968. This view was taken in 1906 and shows the Methodist Church next to the shops on the left. A Methodist congregation was formed in Kirkcaldy in 1883 and this church was built five years later.

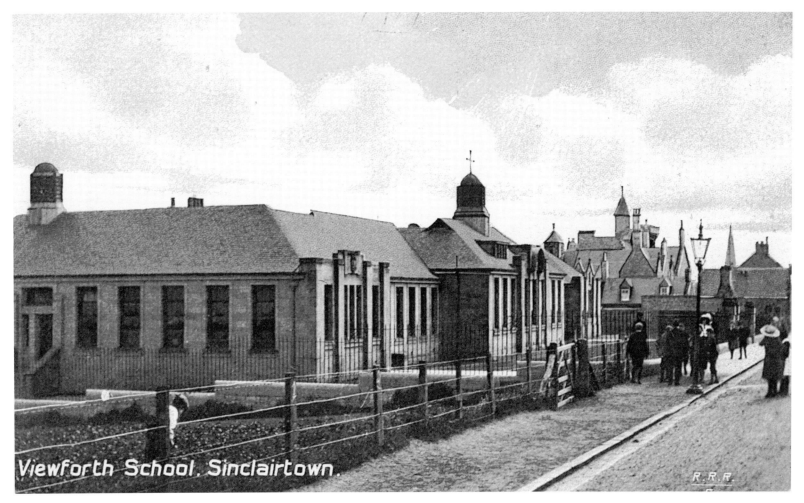

Viewforth School, Sinclairtown.

R.R.R.

When the 1872 Education Act (Scotland) was passed Dysart and Kirkcaldy had some 3,000 pupils between them. By 1920 thirteen new schools had been built and the number of pupils had risen to 8,000. Viewforth School in Loughborough Road was built in 1908 and designed by D. Forbes Smith. It remained a junior secondary, teaching pupils up to the age of sixteen only, until it achieved full secondary school status in 1980.

Overton Road, Kirkcaldy.

Only the former premises of the Pathhead Co-op, on the left of this atmospheric 1930s picture, escaped the bulldozers in the late 1960s. Overton Road derives its name from the Overtoun, one of two small farming settlements (the other being known as the Nethertoun) which predated the feuing of the village of Pathhead.

44

The creation of privately built turnpike roads, made profitable by the imposition of tolls, did much to improve trade and communication in Fife during the late eighteenth century. In 1790 an Act of Parliament authorised the development of two such roads passing through Kirkcaldy; the first from Pettycur to Cupar, where two other roads led to the Tay ferries at Woodhaven and Newport; and the second from Kirkcaldy to Crail via Cameron Bridge. Both roads passed along St Clair Street and Rosslyn Street and by the mid-nineteenth century a continuous ribbon of development along the margins of the turnpike completely joined Pathhead, Sinclairtown and Gallatown. This view of Rosslyn Street dates from around 1910 and shows a few of the surviving buildings in this decimated area.

The 'Galton' - locals never pronounce the second 'a' - is traditionally said to take its name from the location of the parish gallows. The village grew steadily after the introduction of handloom weaving in the early eighteenth century. In 1756 it contained 203 souls; the number had risen to 432 in 1792 and 1,053 by 1836. Like Pathhead, Gallatown was a centre for nail making and in 1792 it was reported that there were forty-three smiths, but that many were advanced in life. The industry had all but ceased by the 1830s. This 1906 view of Rosslyn Street shows a Kirkcaldy Corporation tramcar. The cars were liveried in dark green and ran between termini at Linktown and Gallatown from 1903 until competition from buses led to the withdrawal of the service in 1931.

Rosslyn Street, Gallatown, Kirkcaldy

Today not a stone remains of the buildings in this 1907 view showing a Wemyss and District Tramway car about to turn into Randolph Road on its way to Leven. Unlike the Kirkcaldy tramway, which was a municipal undertaking, the Wemyss tramway was privately developed by Randolph Wemyss of Wemyss Castle. All the Wemyss trams were single deckers and were originally painted a muddy yellow, which earned them the apt nickname of 'mustard boxes', a title which persisted even after the colour scheme was changed to maroon in 1913. The last Wemyss tramcars ran in 1932.

WEMYSS & DISTRICT TRAMWAY, GALLATOWN TERMINUS.

Randolph Road looking east. The picture was probably taken on 4 August 1906, the first day of running of the Wemyss trams. The dilapidated cottage on the right was a tollhouse, built on the new turnpike road in 1792. There was considerable opposition to the toll system and on several occasions while the cottage was being built local people tore parts of it down under the cover of darkness. Eventually the trustees of the road placed a guard of constables around it, but two nights later on 12 December 1792 they were attacked by a mob who pelted them with a barrage of stones. The guards were chased from the village, finding not one house willing to offer them shelter, and the mob demolished the cottage completely. Despite this setback, the Gallatown Toll was eventually accepted and remained in force until all Fife road tolls were abolished in 1878.